GOD'S HAPPY HELPERS

THE STORY OF TABITHA AND FRIENDS

By Marilyn Lashbrook

Illustrated by Stephanie McFetridge Britt

CANDLE
BOOKS

"God's Happy Helpers" tells the story of God's work in the lives of Tabitha and her friends. Your child will see that each believer, big or small, has an important place in the church. And your little one will have fun thinking about ways he or she can serve God.

Pause and allow your child to point to the appropriate picture in answer to each question on pages 7-13. Assure them, God has a special job for them to do too.

First published in the UK in 1996 by Candle Books
(a publishing imprint of Lion Hudson plc).
This printing 2004

Distributed by Marston Book Services Ltd,
PO Box 269, Abingdon, Oxon OX14 4YN

Co-edition arranged by Lion Hudson plc, Oxford

All enquiries to Lion Hudson plc, Mayfield House,
256 Banbury Road, Oxford OX2 7DH

Tel: +44 (0) 1865 302750
Fax: +44 (0) 1865 302757
Email: coed@lionhudson.com
www.lionhudson.com

Printed in Hong Kong

ISBN 1 85985 105 3

GOD'S HAPPY HELPERS

THE STORY OF TABITHA AND FRIENDS

By Marilyn Lashbrook

Illustrated by Stephanie McFetridge Britt

Taken from Acts 9

Here, there, and everywhere; Peter told people about Jesus.

Here, there, and everywhere; people believed.

And one of those people was Tabitha. God gave Tabitha a new life . . . and a new love for people . . . and a new talent to use for Him.

People who believe in Jesus come in all shapes and sizes and ages. Each one has a special job to do.

Some are music makers and some are cookie bakers. Can you find the music makers in the picture? Where are the cookie bakers? Would you rather be a music maker or a cookie baker?

Where are the joyful singers?
Can you find the helpful bringers?
Do you enjoy singing and bringing?

Do you see a Gospel Preacher? Do you see a
Bible teacher? Have you ever pretended to be
a teacher or a preacher?

Greeters, smilers, come-visit-awhilers.
Which of these people is doing something
you like to do?

Each believer has a job to do. Tabitha was a clothing-sewer and kindness-shower. She measured and snipped and stitched; making beautiful clothing for the poor.

When people were sick, Tabitha came to take care of them.

But one day Tabitha got sick. She grew weaker and weaker. And then kind Tabitha died.

Everyone was very sad when she died. Tabitha had shown God's love to many people by her giving and caring.

The get-up-and-goers left the by-her-side–
sitters and went to look for Peter. The
peek-a-boo-players joined the on-their-knees-
prayers to ask God for a miracle.

When Peter heard about Tabitha, he came right away. He hurried up the stairs to Tabitha's room.

"Look what she made us," the poor widows cried. Then they showed Peter their beautiful robes.

"Go downstairs," Peter told them.

He kneeled and prayed. And then he turned
to Tabitha. "Tabitha, get up!" Peter said.

Suddenly, Tabitha opened her eyes and sat up!
She was alive. God had done a miracle!

Peter opened the door. "Come here," he called to the people waiting downstairs. Up the stairs they hurried to see their dear friend.

The room was filled with rejoicers and praisers. The people were so glad to see Tabitha alive. And Tabitha was glad to be alive so she could go on helping others.

The Good-News-Sharers spread the word, and soon the whole town was talking about the wonderful miracle God had done.

Many people believed in Jesus.

Then there were more sharers and carers, singers and bringers, preachers and teachers. Each was given a special talent for sharing God's love with others.

ME TOO!® BOOKS